A
STRAIGHTFORWARD GUIDE
TO
WRITING PERFORMANCE
POETRY

Stephen Wade

Straightforward Publishing
www.straightforwardco.co.uk

Straightforward Publishing
Brighton BN2 4EG

© Stephen Wade 2007

ISBN 1847160 17 4
ISBN 13: 9781847160171

Printed by Biddles Ltd Kings Lynn Norfolk

Cover design by Bookworks Islington

Whilst every effort has been taken to ensure that the
information in this book is correct at the time of going to
press, the author and the publisher cannot accept liability
for any errors and omissions contained within.

CONTENTS

....

Chapter 3

....

Chapter 4

Chapter 5

....

Chapter 8

Working with Others   **83**

....

Chapter 9

Organising yourself   **91**

....

....

INTRODUCTION

In recent years, there has been a definite rise in the numbers of poets who have extended their writing interests and working methods into performance, rather than keeping to the 'page poetry' of meditation, or poems of love, faith, social commentary and so on. Much of this writing has been with comedy-poetry crossover in mind. But there has been very little in print which might supply some guidance and advice.

My involvement in organising poetry events, and in giving readings, has taught me that most failure in performance is due to delivery and preparation rather than to the actual poetic material being read. It has also become clear that the audience for poetry readings is growing (and changing) and that it is no longer satisfactory to stand up and read poems, expecting no audience rapport or interplay.

For these reasons, it seemed necessary to make a start and write something that will help you if you have picked up this book out of curiosity. We live in an age when poetry is no longer a part of that Romantic image of the lonely writer of genius in a garret. Performing poetry has become a central part of the comedy, mass media and literature scene, easily observed at any literature festival, book week or arts fair. It is an art form that is also making space for itself on radio, too. Popular programmes such as *Stanza* and *Poetry Please* on Radio 4 indicate the diversity of subjects and approaches possible to anyone interested in writing poetry for performance.

This book will provide you with advice on the special kind of writing needed here, details of organisational ability needed and techniques of improving delivery and voice projection. The idea behind this is that you may be led to consider extending your range if you are already a well-established poet, or that, if you are a beginner, this may be a short introduction to what is surely one of the most exciting developments in poetry in recent times.

As I write this, I note that on radio this week is (a) a series of readings of poems specifically written for radio by Peter Reading, Kathleen Jamie and Tom Paulin; Murray Lachlan Young has performed on the Paul Ross Show, *The Guardian* has printed a long feature on poetry bohemia, and my Artscene diary for Yorkshire events features no fewer than twelve poetry events in clubs, pubs and arts centres.

1

PUTTING PERFORMANCE POETRY IN CONTEXT

Historical Survey

In a sense, there has been performance poetry ever since there was poetry itself. In English literature, it is well documented that the Anglo-Saxon epic *Beowulf,* for instance, was read aloud to an audience (c.1, 000 A.D.) and the medieval poets would certainly have written with recitation in mind. The idea that poetry is an art which involves writing a lyric for an unknown reader who will read the text alone is a comparatively new idea.

Even in the nineteenth century, when we often think of a context of lonely meditation and academic approaches to poetry, there was a massive interest in 'penny readings' at which workingmen and women would listen to performances of poetry and prose, with material ranging from the classic texts to popular ballads.

Poetry writing has always reflected a variety of conflicting traditions in our society, and the 'town and gown' issue may still be there. But all literature has contained aspects of the popular in some way and often relates to some elements of 'oral tradition' and the poetry recitals and readings of coteries may well be best suited to looking for a wider audience and might even need to be existing alongside more democratic, open and flexible forms of poetry as a social discourse and as a mediation of new urban voices: rap together with 'page' poems.

A fresh approach now

Poets today are increasingly open to developing their work with a specific audience or mode of delivery in mind. They are also interested in linking poetry to other arts. The nature of pop lyrics for instance, has often been compared to poetry as conventionally conceived, and the Poetry Olympics in November 1995 brought together singers, poets, musicians and song-writers in a way that blurred distinctions between the traditional poetry reading and the song performance. After all, a lyric by Ray Davies or Bob Dylan has most of the verbal elements expected in a lyric poem by a typical modern 'page' poet.

To understand what has happened to our conceptions of poetry in recent years, it is useful to reflect on how poetry has been culturally situated in English culture in the twentieth century. Consider, for instance, two countries of the Third World with notions of poetry, which are alien to us. In Colombia, for instance, a huge poetry festival is held annually; poets from all over the world read. There are readings in a massive stadium, and the poetry is in some way a response to the dehumanising powers of drug-culture and universal crime. In Somalia, poetry is broadcast on the radio every day; many ordinary people write poems. There are no connotations of snobbery or elitism such as we have suffered here.

Page and Voice

There was undoubtedly a 1960s revolution in the writing of poetry for voice rather than for academic, fixed on the page reading. The Mersey Poets and Michael Horovitz, together with the performance innovations of Jeff Nuttall, all brought about a need to revise opinions as what exactly poetry was. The tradition of defining poetry only in an academic way was hard to shift. By that decade, we had become accustomed to *studying* poetry. It had become one of the foundations of literary culture as established in the English Literature examinations in school, and in university-based study.

The poets of the Sixties wanted to change the way in which poetry was defined and produced. In the USA it had already been linked to music and to religious thought, and poets such as Allen Ginsberg and Kenneth Rexroth had promoted the idea of performance in more relaxed, strictly non-academic milieus.

'Page' poetry was seen has having certain limitations:

- Linked with serious philosophy

- Written with the use of private reference

- Presented elaborate syntax

- Used obscure vocabulary and imagery

Poets wanted to write in a way that was more flexible, and also in a communal sense, with a feeling for an audience that was not necessarily well-read in poetry of the past, nor likely to listen to poetry in a way that employed analysis.

Performance Poetry - A Map of Origins
Oral tradition/folk song

ballads
recitations and penny readings

music hall/vaudeville

divergence

page (academic) voice   (popular forms)

contemporary media
art in a post-modern context

If you want to be a part of this revolution, where do you start? Obviously, you start with acquiring the essential knowledge. Then there are various options open to you, depending on your personal career aims and your individual interests. Poetry is an art-form with a wide diversity of forms and styles, each with its own audience, much the same as in pop music, where categories are placed on certain bands or concepts.

Essential reading
The first task, before considering options of writing, is to read widely. This would be a constructive and relevant checklist of areas to read and absorb:

18

1. The current poetry magazines, notably *Poetry Review, Agenda, PN Review* and *Stand.* See the booklist for details.
2. Cultural commentaries, such as the crossover reviews: music magazines review such performers as Ivor Cutler, John Hegley and Murray Lachlan Young.
3. Collections and discs by well-known performers.

You need to go to as many performances and readings as possible, and to reflect on what makes for success, what part the audience plays and so on.

Your Options
If you decide to take this seriously and actually learn to write for performance, then you have to give some thought to these possible routes to success:

• Stand-Up Poetry in clubs

• The more literary focus: arts centres, universities etc.

• Traditional readings - not strictly performance.

• Working with other media- for radio perhaps

• Linking poetry with music

All these provide different satisfactions when you reach professional levels of competence, but a great deal depends on what sort of person you are and what background you have in poetry. Most poets seem to be quite happy writing poems for a range of small magazines, never really doing any readings at all. But consider what potential there is in changing attitudes. A typical poet who has been writing for about five years might have the following profile:

1. Achievement: steady trickle of poems in small magazines, occasional success with a London -based magazine.
2 Has qualifications in English. Perhaps done some teaching etc.
3. The first collection has not materialised: the work is not distinctive enough.
4. No other activities tried as yet - editing, working in schools etc.

This is fairly average. There is room for improvement here, if the writer has any real hunger for success. If someone writes poetry, then surely the point is to communicate to as many people as possible? We live in an age of mass media. Poets should thrive now. This is where performance comes in.

The options are therefore concerned with your decisions about how much you are prepared to change. Do you wish to learn techniques of actually giving dramatic presence to your delivery? Do you want to create a character - a stage alter ego? Whichever approach you choose, the fundamentals of the writing will be the same.

The possibilities listed above can only be studied and acted upon if you have thought long and hard about yourself as a writer. Performance involves three basic qualities, and you have to be sure that you can learn them:

1.   Confidence: in your ability and in the quality of your writing.
2.   Sensitivity to audience
3.   A mix of humour and definite thematic material.

On top of these there are delivery and projection skills, but anyone can learn these if the confidence and self-belief are there. The average poetry-lover who attends readings will be patient, and will not expect any startling dramatic ability. He or she will have been to dozens of readings which involve nothing more than the poet standing up and introducing a poem, then reading the poem, and repeating that pattern for an hour's delivery. Most poets who really plan and structure their work will improve on that mediocrity.

Your choice, then, depends on how far you want to take the dramatic element in what you do. The range is as follows:

- Total creation of a character

- An adopted voice and attitude

- A straight address and rapport

The first is virtually stand-up expertise. If your poetry involves humour, satire, local dialect, spoof etc., then this may be for you. The courage required to risk failure is considerable, but the successes are immense and very rewarding. Performers such as Hovis Presley, Ian McMillan and John Hegley have shown the way here.

The second is simply using an accent or a blend of humour. The simplest example of this is the dialect recital. A poet who writes in local dialect has all the resources and qualities of that verbal richness as a resource, from the very first line. The classic example of this is the comic monologue, as in Stanley Holloway's *Albert* poems.

The last is the most common, and for this to succeed, all the power and variety has to be in the words and structures of rhythm, rhyme and sound effects. In other words, the writing has to be immediately understandable, but rich in inherent humour or emotive quality, so that the listener can respond quickly and not need your presence other than as a clear and attractive voice.

Now read the Key Points from Chapter One.

KEY POINTS FROM CHAPTER ONE

PUTTING PERFORMANCE POETRY IN CONTEXT

- Understand the conventions and established forms, then choose your preference

- Learn by watching performers and by reading widely

- Decide on your subjects and themes with regard to delivery and spoken poetry

- Adopt and practise skills and styles which are urgently contemporary

Now turn to Chapter Two

2

MONITORING THE PREPARATION REQUIRED

Your important decisions

If you have given some thought to the fundamental issues raised in the first chapter, you should now be ready to assess what resources for writing performance poetry you have now, before any skills work is approached. These resources may be understood in terms of three areas of potential ability:

1. Your skill in expressing yourself clearly
2. An ability to project interest through language
3. A desire to entertain, more than to inform.

It does not really matter whether or not you have a background in theatre work. If you do or have done work that involves public speaking, then obviously that is advantageous. But the heart of this genre of poetry is the need to express stories and ideas communally. It is a sharing poetry, an art of defining togetherness and describing a version of a corporate enterprise- life.

What assets are universal?

In all writing, there is a certain body of 'material' which is a reliable resource if you can access it. This is your own specific experience on life. If you can create an angle, a viewpoint, on that experience, then you can create stories or provide commentaries, which will be irresistible in performance. Take, for instance, the experience of school. This subject has been dealt with in countless memoirs, comic novels, stand-up routines and songs. Consider your own schooling and note down what makes it unique but also what makes it expressive of the experience of a class/generation etc.

Creating material for poetry from a range of experience or observation is similar to the process of preparing a monologue; you have to consider the topic itself, together with a 'patter' - a talking around the subject, however briefly. You are the only person who can develop a performance repertoire in this way about individual experience.

A first checklist
Start with a list of your own subjects - the areas of life and observation that you could write and talk about. Most of us would include such things as childhood, friends, teachers, games, achievements, relatives, games/hobbies/passions/obsessions and so on. Do your own checklist and then pick out the top six. Look for linking themes which unite these six. It might be your own learning experience or it might be a friend.

This is the first list of *raw material* from which to work and write.

At this point, it is important to pause and look a little more closely at what exactly this art form is. Performance poetry is essentially the reading and presentation of poetic material which is primarily meant for reading aloud to an audience, rather than for the private reading of a poem by one reader. This is simple but all-inclusive. However, what it does not tell you is that performance is also an element involving far more than simply *reading aloud*.

In the conventional poetry reading, in academic circles or in writers' groups, the established process is for the poet to talk about the experience which lies at the basis of the poem's subject, then to read the poem with the rhythms intended by the syntax, layout and other verbal devices. Performance is another skill entirely.

Explaining the performance element
In addition to the 'reading aloud' involved, consider the range of other, related and very necessary skills involved in being a poetry performer. All these should be part of any definition:

• Being able to deliver the meaning clearly

• Having the skill to relate body movement to language

• Modulation and control of the voice

• Acute awareness of the audience
  Defining performance poetry, therefore, becomes less straightforward the more one reflects on the nature of

the process involved. But performance and reading have become inter-related and have fused into any situation in which one person reads aloud to an audience. However, most poets who call themselves 'performers' would surely claim to have developed a strongly individual technique of delivery. There is a factor X which can only be observed by its difference rather than by common definition.

For instance, many people have commented that a poet's work looks simple and very weak 'on the page' yet when delivered and read aloud seems to be transformed into something different. Much of Roger McGough's work may look slender and in some ways 'unpoetic' on the page, but in performance there is a sea-change into something' rich and strange'.

Rhythm and structure

One of the fascinating aspects of writing poetry is that there is some kind of inner, directing sense of rhythm and structure which dictates the way you develop your writing. There are controlling devices in the creative brain which somehow tell the writer when and how to use certain rhythms, punctuation, word selection and so on. But the intense focus on poetry written for the page, to be read privately, has meant that our culture has a strict, academic definition of poetry which involves certain elements of composition. It is worth thinking about these features before discussing how 'voice' poetry differs from 'page' poetry. The features could be expressed like this:

'Page poetry' involves

1.   Writing with a strong sense of conventional approaches. e.g. rhyme scheme and
    patterns of imagery.

2. Sharing a meditational, inner lyric 'I' with one reader.

3.   Indulging in personal, individuated expression of experience

4. Being uninfluenced by any need to appeal to communal or societal experience.

5. Taking it for granted that poetry in this form needs to be explained and studied.

6. Accepting the special nature of the discourse of poetry as distant from colloquial talk.

Reflect on the features above, and note that this version of poetry is very restrictive. It defines the art by insisting that there is a social value in the individual response to the world. There is a tradition of accepting a poetic statement as somehow sacral, distinctively wise, taken as a variety of philosophical writing.

Romantic aesthetics

'Page' poetry in our culture has also been influenced, by means of the mediation of poetry as somehow exclusive and elitist, by a vulgarised version of the Romantic ideals of relation to nature, childhood, innocence and so on. The persistent influence of 'page' poetry as the defining pattern and model of what 'real' or 'deep' poetry is has been detrimental to the reassertion that poetry is a social art which exists in order to make public the experience we all share at a specific time and in a specific place, and also in our common humanity.

'Voice' poetry - freedom and flexibility

When you write poems to be read aloud, dramatised and performed, you are immediately having to learn a different set of conventions. The basic need, above all else, is a sense of the rhythms of authentic spoken language. Consider the features of speech in everyday usage:

- Unstructured, rambling, lacking fluency

- Does not obey rules of 'correctness'

- Contains features that are regional

- Contains features that are unique to the speaker (idiolects)

- Has a sense of adventure - unplanned, not pre-conceived

- Relies on the situation and on the listener

Note how radical some of these items are when applied to the idea of writing poetry for one private reader. The performance poet has to make the reading of the poem seem authentic, contemporary, fluent and immediately communicative. Footnotes are a total impossibility. There should be no explanation necessary. But, on the other hand, many of the features of actual speech can be written and pre-planned as a stylistic device by the poet. For instance, digressions, repetitions, puns, innuendo and local words would be representative of this trend.

You only have to consider a traditional folk-song to see this. Many folk songs are close to the features of performance poems, of course. A famous song such as 'The Oldham Weaver' (sung by Ewan McColl) makes some demands on the listener who has no knowledge of Lancashire dialect, but most of the contents are self-explanatory.

Your first steps should be in acquiring a knowledge of the best work in this genre. This will involve being aware of the diversity as well. The basic factor of entertainment is still the crucial one, regardless of which poets you study. J.E.Carpenter, writing about Penny Readings in the 1850s recognised this: 'And here we would venture to give the managers of "Penny Readings" a word of friendly advice: if they insist upon giving their audience nothing but dry, serious and 'instructive' matter, they will drive them away by degrees...'

A reading programme
Begin by choosing one representative writer from each of the three main categories. For instance:

1. Literary, serious social commentary etc. e.g. Simon Armitage
2. Comedic, with undertones of commentary e.g. John Hegley
3. Primarily entertainment, with integral 'stand-up' e.g. Ian McMillan
But what you will notice when researching this area is that there are always poets and artists who are

unclassifiable. The above is simply a rule-of-thumb summary of the majority of performers.

Research by doing these types of study:

- Listen to tape recordings of performance and try to relate the words to gesture, movement, changes in tone and subject.

- Read the text of poems, analysing the nature of the stylistic devices such as refrains, puns and so on.

- Above all, note and consider all the linking and introductory ploys used to add interest to the poems.

What you must do is work out your own types of classification in accordance with the poetry you wish to write and perform. This is an example. Supposing you create a certain voice - a reading voice which you adopt when reading your poems. Obviously, reading and recording yourself reading this material will be useful, but first study how an established poet does this. Find a text and a recording of a particular poem, then write a checklist of the ways in which the 'skeleton' of the text becomes the living creature that is alive when read or performed. This is seen most easily with someone like John Betjeman or Pam Ayres, poets who rely on simple end-rhymes for the 'punch' of meaning. Betjeman's recordings, done with musical accompaniment, integrate the cadences of his descriptions and satirical lines with changes in the musical settings. (see *Betjeman's Banana Blush* in the booklist/reference section)

The most benefit is clearly to be gained from a close study of how and why the really popular poets succeed. For instance, in 1997, Murray Lachlan Young was very successful in linking performance poetry with music, but his real talent was clearly in the original delivery and accentuation of his lines, linking words and meanings to body movements and image. Discover your voice's features.

Your Profile of Essential Preparation

Equipment

Tape recorder (portable)

Collection- personal anthology of poems

Checklist of projection techniques

Audio-visual materials

Observation Log

Videos + notes on non-verbal communication

Use and type of music used

Audience rapport - methods used

List of linking methods: anecdotes, jokes, themes etc.

Language Notes

Glossary of comic writing: refer to literary terms and techniques

Index of subjects and index of treatments

Index of cuttings etc. for real-life reference

Now read the Key Points from Chapter Two

KEY POINTS FROM CHAPTER TWO

MONITORING THE PREPARATION REQUIRED

- Study the common factors in all successful performance

- Work on the specific rhythmic elements from the beginning.

- Write a checklist of what makes 'voice' poetry different

- Gather equipment and materials as support resources

Now turn to Chapter Three

3

TAKING THE FIRST STEPS IN WRITING

Finding out what makes a poem for performance

Now that you have done all the important planning and self-questioning, it is time to consider some of the most positive ways to actually start writing for performance. There are a variety of possible approaches here, but the most reliable, as in all forms of writing, is to consider the structure and language of a poem which has been read and delivered to a live audience. Remember that the first criterion of the form is that the poem should be written with *oral delivery* in mind. It is to be *spoken* aloud, with a sense of audience.

If you have read widely as part of your preparation for writing, and also as a central focus for your learning process as a poet, you will be familiar with a range of poems written for this genre, but instead of taking a classic, here is a poem which has been read aloud perhaps a dozen times at poetry readings, but has to definitive printed form. That is, it has not appeared in a collection (only in an anthology). Here is the full text:

> 'I Read and Sigh'
> 9 a.m.
> I fill the satchel with paper.

I walk past a man.
His briefcase is full of paper.
He walks past another man,
burdened also with the weight of hope.
But we do not smile.
4 p.m.
I fill the satchel with different paper.
I walk past the man again.
He has a briefcase full of paper
and he carries other paper.
But still we do not smile.
6 p.m.
I load the kitchen table with paper.
I see this other man, reading paper.
He may be dad, but we do not smile.
I read geographical terms.
I read about the plight of rainforests.
We both place quantities of paper in our bin.
'Happy tree' I wish him.
But he does not smile,
And I want my 'A' level geography.
'I read and sigh and wish I were a tree'
Do you read me?

There are several features of this which illustrate the nature of a performance poem. Note that in the style there are these techniques:

- Little use of linking words

- Repetition of pronouns without combining sentences

- Use of parallel phrases and repetitions

- A mixture of childish and formal language

The poem aims to state a very simple observation with a most unsubtle irony. In fact, there is nothing obvious here except an insistent theme of social comment about a society reliant on paper and on the destruction of nature. Performance poetry allows this kind of direct address, allowing the subject to develop without having to be construed or deconstructed by criticism. It should be as plain as a song-lyric, proclaiming what it is 'about' with immediacy and appeal to both emotion and reason.

Yet under the plainness there is a subtle technique, involving two outstanding and rhetorical devices: First, a staging of events in a mini-narrative, and second, a sequence of undercurrent comment - in this case, the fact that the people in the poem do not speak. Therefore, the poem works in this way:

Level one: surface. The overt theme of social commentary - the 'green' issue.
Level two: drama/narrative. A story is told in glimpses (scenes)
Level three: Undercurrent or parallel theme. Another topic is dealt with, inviting comparison or linking of the surface with the undercurrent ideas.

Delivery
In addition to all this, there is the element which is added purely as a spoken characteristic- the delivery.

Before the poem is read aloud, the punctuation, repetitions and other devices ask the listener to note the 'changes of gear' in terms of how the material is delivered.

This is where your own sense of a spoken delivery plays a part. There is no way to learn an artificial presentation. You have to work on the sense of the inner voice, which dictated the poem when it was written. But there are some techniques to help you. The point is that your poem is to be read, to be dramatic and to hold the attention of people who *cannot see the text*. You must therefore use markers and links to add a sense of direction and story to the voice.

Marker:
This is often a word used to define, such as a *determiner*: this, one, each etc. But it may also be a number or an emphatic word which you are repeating for stylistic reasons.
Links:
A link is obviously a word, which makes it clear to the listener that a stage has been reached and another focus or subject is on the way. Words denoting time would be an obvious example.

But your voice is at the heart of this, and you must know its tones and attitudes well. One of the best ways to know what voice habits you have is to record yourself reading one of your own poems, or any standard performance poem, and apply adjectives to the tone you hear. If you have people who will listen objectively and supply adjectives, that is clearly very profitable too. Words such as *sarcastic, cynical, innocent, dramatic, monotone, angry* etc. are what you want here. The reason for this being so important is that we write automatically, without a sense of the spoken voice. Instead, we hear a controlling 'voice' inside the head, a quiet interior control that ensures that your sentences and phrases are acceptable in idiom, authenticity and register. Note the importance of these as you listen to your voice:

idiom is concerned with the contemporary nature of your words - a way of speaking that relates you to your social context and peers.

authenticity is that factor which signifies to the listener that you are a language-user of his or her time, context and nature. Nothing in your poem should 'jar' on the reader's ear.

register relates a particular use of language to a given situation. If you write a poem in the form of a supposed letter, then your words, sentences and syntax should be that of a letter, as your audience conceives of such a thing.

Do the voice is at the centre, controlling all this. How do we feel sure that we have the kind of voice we aim at as a performer? Surely, as with all good writing, the main source is observation of life. We speak after learning by listening. Mimicry goes deeper than a surface feature that gets a laugh.

The voice you adopt when reading a poem aloud betrays three significant aspects of you and your view of the world:

- The degree to which you question or accept things

- The place of formality/informality in your perspective

- Your involvement or detachment from your subjects.

If these aspects are noted, then consider how important it is to control your delivery with extreme care. If you have never listened to public speakers before, then start doing so now. Note and observe all kinds of people who have to live by speaking clearly to audiences, and make a log of comments and responses on what they do and how they use language. You might include in your list lecturers, comedians, politicians, actors, journalists or even market tradesmen- 'grafters' who hold an audience. There are several obvious but not commonly absorbed techniques, which such professions have adopted. They are all to do with three crucial objectives:

1. Interest your listener immediately.
2. Hold that interest.
3. Modulate and direct your voice with gesture and movement.

In classical Greek and Roman culture, and in the European universities of the Renaissance, this was oratory. In other words, experience should teach any performer that your first duty is to be heard and your second to speak what the audience wants to listen to.

Know your own voice

In the case of poetry, it is similar to narrative. Stylistic devices such as repetition and emotive language will play their part, but at the core there is the unavoidable quality of your voice. Learn by listening and watching, adopting and practising as you learn. The only real negative is never be monotone. Every public speaker changes the tone and 'key' along a scale. In poetry reading this is probably more important than in other areas. The poet has to be sure that every word is heard, unlike a singer, who has the music and the rhythms behind the lyric to hold the listener's interest.

Of course, you also have the vast and flexible mass of words in the English language behind you - and here, the point is exactly that: use the resources wherever possible. Just think of some of the immensely valuable literary sources for a poet who writes for performance, all available in classic texts:

- children's stories

- jokes

- limericks and rhymes

- Nonsense poetry

- radio drama

- comic-book narrative

- film dialogue

What these and many others have in common is that a writer can parody or spoof their technique and language. The technical word in cultural studies is *appropriate*. One writer may appropriate all the conventions of language of another form or convention. For a performance poet, this is an infinite resource of words. That is, if you want ideas as to how to charge and invigorate your style, then appropriate another way of telling. Not word for word of course - simply write *in the manner of* some other form. Such a parody will immediately invite you to use language creatively as a spoken medium.

The classic example is to listen to a story being told. Notice that when a skilful teller relates a story, he embellishes as well as gives the basic plot and events. Your poem should do this, and a sensitivity to the spoken language is the only way.

Some useful research skills
Here is a simple way to absorb some spoken forms of language, which will lead into potential performance writing.

Stage one: Walk through a busy place, notebook in hand, and note any spoken or written announcements or talk that is meant for the public. A market is an ideal location.

Stage two: Write a checklist of subjects that you want to write about, then choose one of the discourses you have heard to match the subject.

Stage three: Back in the study, write your first lines in the normal way, and then in the discourse you have heard. For instance, a market trader selling excellent pans and kitchenware might have said:

'Ladies..... invest in something permanent.... stainless and non-stick pans... never let you down......'

Your version might be applied to a love-poem:

Your love, you said, is stainless,
non-stick, but will never let me down......

The important point here is that in writing for performance, always put the everyday and the universal before the abstract and the intellectual. use concrete language, with immediate appeal and sense, and use the resources of English to the full, as a language full of puns and double-meanings, in which even a slightly wrong word will cause a poetic effect. A shop-window has a sign saying 'Managing Women: a one-day Seminar'. The verb 'managing' here applies to no subject, so it could be a course for people who want to manage women, or a course for women who want power.

Now read the Key Points from Chapter Three

KEY POINTS FROM CHAPTER THREE

TAKING THE FIRST STEPS IN WRITING

- Learn to define the composition of a performance poem

- Work on all aspects of clear and interesting delivery

- Be familiar with the features of your voice and work on its effectiveness

- Always listen to and note authentic speech

Now turn to Chapter Four

4

APPLYING WORKING METHODS I

The problem of subjects

In all varieties of writing, there is one working method, which has to be adopted by most writers. With few exceptions, creative writing involves a process of moving from notes on an original idea to a finished, final draft. In between comes the editing, re-thinking and re-writing that are essential to success. With poetry, this is particularly so, as many ideas for poems might be first written as a few random lines taken from observation.

The basic process is this:

1. Observation and notes
2. First lines or images
3. Building a structure

Writing for performance involves much more of this, as you have an audience, which is present. Weaknesses will show, and lines cannot be skipped over rapidly. Every word has to be just right and do some work towards the full communication.

An idea to a draft

Suppose you take as a subject a busy market day in a large town. The real focus is on people, of course. You might start with rough notes on notices, goods on sale, diversity of social types etc., then you need a few key lines or images, which might be the repeated lines or refrains. For instance:

Notes - Friendly Street market - man with old school tie, carrying flowers. Guilt purchase? Man, afro-Yorkshireman, frizzy hair. Thick-rimmed glasses. Suddenly the Caribbean? Flowery shirt and Jamaican accent. Cheap colour print of Johnny and the Hurricanes. Sign above dresses: 'frocks, large sizes, small prices. See the tags!'

Potential ideas From these rough notes there might be potential in these two phrases for your title and/or refrain: *Guilt purchase* and Suddenly *the Caribbean*. I have picked these because they suggest some drama, some irony and some humour with a definite setting.

Draft You might start with working out two rhyming couplets:

> *A guilt purchase his old eyes covet.*
> *Handbag, chocolates? But she'll tell him where to*
> *shove it.*

Your poem might simply stay at the level of description, just listing what you see and not using any other rhymes - just the rhythms your voice works out.

Development

Each element in your draft might be worked on separately, until you feel that you have an authentic feel to the product. What you are looking for, with reading aloud in mind, is something that will give the listener a sense of anticipation and also a familiarity with the rhythm, so that the rhymed lines are expected, but create irony or sarcasm etc.

Using a tape recorder

Many writers find a tape-recorder has several uses in writing for performance. Remember that your first consideration is always the flexibility and versatility of the spoken word. You need to be comfortable with your own delivery of lines. Most people have experienced a sense of dismay when listening to their recorded voice. It is helpful now to think about these:

- a sense of the voice being monotone

- a sensitivity to local / class accent

- awareness of the difficulties of linking words and being fluent

- limitation in the stress and intonation patterns adopted.

For instance, it could be argued that we now live in a society in which conversation and the use of the spoken words in prolonged communication is becoming obsolete. Only in using the voice for specific purposes, with variety of contexts and reasons can we truly get to know our own voice and its characteristics. So the above checklist of dissatisfactions is actually a list of features to be overcome if you want to succeed in reading poetry to an audience. The performance poet needs total ease and familiarity with his or her voice - in terms of capabilities and potential for drama, change of mood, fluency and so on.

Record and vary speech qualities

The aspects of your voice which, in terms of phonology (the study of speech production) are important for delivery and performance are:

- stress patterns

- intonation

- sonority/modulation

- idiolect

- use of the speech chain- articulation

All these may be understood and therefore the knowledge may be applied to your poetry quite easily. Using a tape-recorder will help in this. These are the explanations of each term, with exercises:

stress patterns

This means the way in which certain words or syllables are stressed in English in such a way that meaning is made clear. In reading a poem, you need to be sure that the effects you aim at are helped by using stressed syllables to the full.

Exercise: Read a dozen lines of any classic poem several times, then play back, and note any differences. Also note how you have naturally stressed certain parts of the whole in order to convey poetic effects. Do the same with your own poems.

intonation

This is the overall rise and fall of your voice as you speak. For instance, notice how you say the following sentence (a) normally and (b) showing sarcasm:
You're going to the shop again?

Also, notice how a statement can become a question simply by changing intonation:

You are from Sheffield - having the same meaning as *Are you from Sheffield?*

Exercise: Write and then read aloud three lines of sarcasm or abuse - something emotionally powerful. Then listen, or playback, for where, when and why your voice rises and falls to high or low levels.

Sonority/modulation

These are simply about loudness and strength and also making this strength varied. In other words, consciously practice speaking loudly enough to be heard, and also avoid the dullness of a monotone delivery. Work on intonation and the monotones will disappear.

Exercise: Simply read and record poems, purposely speaking more emphatically than usual, and try to *change gear* from forceful to soft expression, according to context and meaning.

idiolect

This is the word used by linguists for our own individual voice qualities. We each have specific speech habits. Listen very closely to your speech and you will detect certain distinct articulations of certain vowels or consonants in combination. Detect and list these, so that anything that might cause communication to be interfered with might be erased. Or equally, your idiolect might contain pleasing qualities. The only way you can really tell is by asking for responses!

Exercise Read and record a passage for about five minutes. Listen on playback for any speech habits you have which are often repeated and would be obvious to a listener. For instance, you might pronounce 's' very softly or very harshly, or you might pronounce certain diphthongs (vowel combinations) in unusual ways - like 'au' in words like holocaust or trauma - do you say 'or' or 'ow' ?

articulation

What in ordinary speech we call 'clarity' often depends on how you use all the physical elements of the mechanisms of voice production. If you consider all the parts of the body that play a part in the production of an utterance, you have to move from chest, then larynx, to tongue, nose, palate and so on. In other words, if you do not talk clearly, the answer may well be in habits you have acquired which inhibit clarity in expression. This may seem obvious, but many poets have given readings without any thought given to such obvious things. This is quite a technical aspect of phonetics, but in plain English, these are the main problems to be aware of:

1. Not sounding the 't' in the middle of words (butter, matter)
2. Not sounding the 'g' at the end of words such as singing, dancing.
3. Using glottal stops (the grunt-like sound made in the throat giving *innit* for isn't it.
4. Running words together - for instance law and order becoming *loranorder*

All this is nothing to do with snobbery or 'correct' English. It is simply about doing what you can to be heard properly and to say what you mean in a clear way. There is no suggestion that you should eradicate a regional accent, and you can preserve regional or local characteristics, of course, if relevant to what you read.

Exercise Quite simply, read and record, and ask a friend to listen, pointing out the problems.

This is much simpler than the above. The idea of a tone is simply your attitude, which may be created by one of several elements in your poetry:

- the humour

- use of slang

- satire

- local accent

- adopted character or act

A question of tone

Each poem will have a range of tones or even voices. Obviously, if you use dialogue, this is essential, but in every poem, you will need to 'change gear' and adopt poses and attitudes or even write a poem purposefully in different voices. Here is an example of what is often demanded in a performance poem:

Elements:
1. Narrator's voice
2. Dialogue
3. Descriptive setting
4. Metaphorical - heightened element.

It may seem to anyone who is well experienced in reading poetry aloud that this is too elementary, but long experience has shown that many people need to be taught how to read poetry with a range of tones, to express the richness of meaning and feeling. The easiest way to see this is to study an extract from a poem written for reading aloud:

I feel aware of stone,
cream and yellow blocks
bordering the riverbank.
And the high Minster, brooding;
solid in the twilight,
somehow a threat,

This is an extract from a poem dealing with being in a hotel, a safe womb, when in the night outside there has been a murder - and in York, a place associated with culture, tourists, history etc.

To put it simply, a reader needs to change 'pitch' and mood when switching from setting to event, or from emotion to emotion. Here, the word *brooding* in the position at the end of the line, needs special attention, and adds a different mood. Similarly the last line, *somehow a threat*, which has to carry both uncertainty and danger.

In most cases, such subtleties of readings will emerge naturally after several readings. The above remarks are simply to draw attention, for beginners, to the crucially important matter of reading in such a way that intonation matches feeling, and these match the changes of mood or increased tempo as a poem progresses.

Ever since the first ballad poems, spoken poetry has had elements of narrative, and stories seem to need links, formulas which repeat the important stages or statements of the narrative. But in modern performance poetry, there are infinite possibilities. Traditionally, one refrain, such as Dylan's 'Blowin in the wind' chorus, is enough to back up a direct and emphatic statement with a clear form, but what about a poem written in a post-modern climate? Postmodernism is a word that means many things, but part of its meaning is that writing takes place within countless other communications and media, and that genres and literary forms are no longer generally agreed on as 'better' or more proper than others.

The idea of **free verse** is a part of this. Set poetic forms no longer dictate how poetry should be written. A performance poem can use supporting media, or explore inner psychological meanings, play around with time reference and so on. So now a refrain or repetition can be an even more powerful tool than in earlier, formal poetry. In a formal 'page' poem such as Edmund Spenser's marriage celebration, *Prothalamion,* the repeated line is 'Sweet Thames run softly till I end my song'. Now, this adds a mood and is aesthetically pleasant in itself, in its cadences. But in a modern performance poem, there are limitless ways to use repetition. For instance:

- as a haunting, nagging insistent doubt

- as a sarcastic or ironical device

- to add a sharp contrast

- to give a new tone or attitude

- to relate to time-shift

This could be extended, and particularly if we include poems for radio or film, the potential expands further (see Tony Harrison's poem V for instance) But in most cases, a refrain or repetition still works as a beat, a rhythm, a unifying agent which links elements and gives a 'punch' of meaning. Interesting examples are Adrian Henri's *I want to paint* used at the beginning of each stanza, or the famous and much-anthologised *I like that stuff* by Adrian Mitchell. (see booklets)

THE DRAFTING/EDITING PROCESS

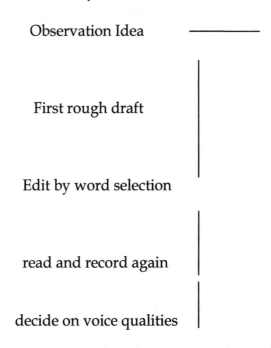

Observation Idea

First rough draft

Edit by word selection

read and record again

decide on voice qualities

Clearly, everyone works out a particular *modus operandi*, and in most cases, it may only be a case of the traditional problem of changing habits. Many writers work themselves into routines and habits of thought which will perhaps not be suited to the needs of breaking out into new forms of mediation. Imagine what a wrench it is to transfer from a private meditational and lyric art to one that, while essentially dealing with the same themes

54

and concerns, has to shift into the area of public sharing, open commentary and assuming the role of community *makkar*: you are proclaiming 'I am a craftsman in the art of poetry, and my verses assert our sharing of humanity. No exclusiveness here'.

Now read the Key Points from Chapter Four

KEY POINTS FROM CHAPTER FOUR

APPLYING WORKING METHODS I

- Always use a system of gathering and developing new subjects -from life

- Work from quickly done drafts to final drafts, and with great care.

- Use recording and editing for capturing convincing tone and syntax

- Try a range of attitudes and tones - even within one subject or theme

Now turn to Chapter Five

5

APPLYING WORKING METHODS

2

The move towards planning a performance also includes a great deal of work on the areas of supporting materials 'around' the text. It might be linking between items, or developing a theme. This section looks at some possibilities here, and also covers some aspects of delivery and reading.

Acquiring supporting skills

The secret of rapport with an audience is first of all to establish what an audience at a specific venue wants. Clearly, there are local differences and also differences in to what extent the audience is familiar with your work generally. But what matters is that you allow for the 'set' of poems and links to be professional, well worked and integrated, and yet also 'natural'. A reading should come across as being the first reading -every time. This is where the support comes in. These are some ideas:
alternating serious and light

poet-comedian, such as Hovis Presley, uses very short jokes, double-entendres and puns in between the poems with the more serious social commentary. Equally, if one studies John Hegley's poetry, there are important comments given on relationships, the need for efforts at understanding, education and so on, in between the songs and rapid-fire gags.

Using autobiographical material

As so many poems are based on people, events and places which were originally personal experience of the writer, why not use 'talking around' the poem by making bold or even surreal statements about the people in or linked to the poem? For instance, in one of my own creations for performance, my Uncle Albert, I extended his character into a persona known as J.Arthur Bowler, and he in introduced in this way:

J.Arthur Bowler: Poetry as Chelping on

When a great poet has come amongst you, you shall know him by this sign: he wears a grey waistcoat and hears voices in his head. The time is now right for the Voice to come forth from Yorkshire. With a pedigree reaching back across eras of poetic creation, as least as far as Willis 'the Pain' Bowler of Cleckheaton, he has arrived, impressively, on a number 36 bus...'

In other words, there is a need for the poems to exist in a setting, a potentially fictional or narrative one, much as a stand-up comic will re-introduce characters by name and by immediate tags of identity such as catch-phrases, walks, clothes etc.

Songs, movement, variety etc.

You might want to introduce other, contrasting items which set the poems apart. Audience chat, digression, acting the fool - these are all well-established devices. But sung versions of poems, or even dialogues with another performer would work well. A useful device, if you have no singing-voice or musical elements, is to read a monologue in which a friend in the audience participates. A short story, in the first person, with dramatised dialogue interworked, with the other participant in the audience, is ideal for a small-scale performance as in a club or art centre.

Developing a character

Obviously, if you want to go beyond a simple reading of poems and add some drama and projection of humour, you need to work on a character: to create a persona. Most are developed from real people, from the poet's observation of life, and sometimes from eccentrics and 'true originals'. The best way to give an account of this is to summarise the work done on a character used in a few local performances in a North of England context.

This was the invention of a poet called Dimitri Todgeroff. I wanted to say something about the status of art and poetry in the north, with a working-class context in mind. Poetry has the negativity of being effeminate and twee in many social contexts. So I made by poet a pretend -Russian. He writes about Batley as if it were Soviet Russia. The elements in him came from local readings, particularly one to an audience of about fifty people in a Chinese restaurant, when I realised that he had to bellow, to shout the poems. Otherwise, the recipe was:

a *Russian accent much-overdone.*
a bullying and aggressive attitude
an obsession with sex pretending to be a tenderness for 'ladies'

If one asks, how is such a character worked on? Usually, it starts with a few mumblings by oneself, working on the voice, then trying out clothes that would be suitable - and finally the trial run. It took three appearances by Todgeroff to find out if it was actually funny to others, as opposed to oneself.

Naturally, logging notes from observation and using photographs are useful supporting techniques as well, but the interest by the poet in the known subject is the deciding factor. As always with such things, it is also crucially important to watch and study the successful examples - even as far back as Hancock, Steptoe and so on.

Linking and patter

I would like to stay with this character in order to say some things about the wrapping around of your poems with other types of discourse. I suggest the following elements:

introduction
one-liner links
digressions (maybe even adlibs)

Introductions: with Todgeroff, it was a case of wanting to relate his poems to a working-class Leeds context. I imagined him as a lad from an estate who found poetry. My introduction used this background:

Ladies and gentlemen, what chance has a poet got in Yorkshire? I know I once said to my dad, 'Dad. I'm going to be a great poet like Byron..' He told me not to say that to anyone outside the house or he'd be sent to Coventry. I asked him was that where Lord Byron lived?

The one-liner links are often simply notes on the implications on what has been read. For instance, Todgeroff reads a poem about a woman with a moustache. My links might be:

Hitler would have liked her or *She thought electrolysis was a new idea in supermarket shopping.*

Really, with performance poetry of the more established, traditional kind, anything will do as long as it breaks the flow of poems. In the worst kind of poetry reading - the one where every poem is introduced at great length and the audience is expected to follow a lecture about the sources of the idea- is not dead, but is slowly dying and will inevitably go, one hopes, for ever.

'Patter' is perhaps impossible to teach and can only be natural. If you want to concentrate on the poetry and keep all commentary to a minimum, then play it safe and simply add sarcastic or self-undermining comments. An audience will enjoy gentle ridicule and undermining of the person before them. A common ploy is to use one's childish nature from the past. Inane and simple comments on what has been read often work well.

My practice is actually to write a few lines of patter and learn them. For instance, my J.Arthur Bowler character involves hypochondria, and I have lines such as these between poems:

Arthur went to see the doctor. He said he was having difficulties with sex. 'Infrequent?' the doctor asked. 'Never.' Arthur said with a sigh.

As with so much writing in many categories and genres, poetry-performance involves a need for a constant source of contemporary comments and newspapers are the best sources. For example, I read a story about some sheep-farmers who put the word 'Heft' on a feedback sheet for some veterinary researcher. He was puzzled as to the nature of this disease. It turned out that it was a shorthand in that area for 'Has every f...... thing...'

Planning a Set
Your performance will usually be somewhere between twenty minutes and half an hour. Supposing you start by doing a gig at a student event, and the venue is a union bar or a common room, or in an arts centre. You will be one of a string of acts. If you want to maximise the possibility of further bookings, make these smooth, entertaining, and never solemn. No poems about inner tragedies. Play it safe and keep to communal, social, political topics or absolutely universal 'eternal verities'.

Of course, it is also possible to have a set which is totally surreal, inane and wild. No problems with that at all.

These are the elements which make a set successful:

- awareness of the audience, setting and locale

- no over-extended pieces

- variety

- pace and fluency

Awareness

This is your sensitivity to the audience and your use of any research or 'feel' about the place where you are. Clearly, an active response to and close observation of the environment and the mood of the place will help here. But if your material is universal and immediate, there will be no problems. The words you here as you mix and observe before the performance will be helpful.

Length

I once went to a reading in which a poet read a poem which lasted for twenty minutes. It was not a poem about universal experience. In fact, it was on a regional, historical topic. The audience had to concentrate closely all the time, trying to be sure of references and dialect terms and so on. The lesson is obvious. Short poems with a definite kick, a well-pointed subject, do best when read aloud or actively, dramatically performed. A lyric, meditative poem will maybe take three minutes to read on average. A useful gauge for a twenty-minute set would be:

6 short lyrics - 12 minutes
1 longer piece - 4 minutes
links / intro. - 2 minutes

Variety
This should be self-evident in all discussions of performance, but I have attended several readings at which people have read, say, four poems about the death of a son, in sequence. Now, that is quite valid in one sense, but in general terms, the whole problem of the subject for performance poetry is not openly discussed. Rather cynically, one has to say that an audience will not really welcome a whole performance based on such dominating, all- consuming emotions as loss, bereavement etc. The most powerful way to read about such things is to place one poem on the subject in a set of ten others dealing with less heavy, severe, personal topics. Douglas Dunn's poems on the death of his wife, *Elegies*, are wonderful poetic statements, but one has to ask what would be gained if they were read aloud as opposed to being read on the page.

So the guidelines are: choose a set which ranges over at least four different subjects in a twenty-minute set, and try to have more than one overall theme.

Pace is vitally important. In simple terms, vary the tempo according to the length, the subject and the emotional focus. Supposing you have three poems towards the end of the reading, and the last poem is a very poignant, resonant topic. Lead up to in with contrast and allow any response to settle before reading. Equally, be steady and thoughtful when leading up to a poem with a strong emotional centre. Any poem that needs a short silence after reading should be placed in the sequence so that you have maximum effect. All this is common sense, but this advice will avoid any mistakes:

1. Choose the order of reading with care.
2. time the longer poems and vary the readings - adding a slower pace to fit the mood etc.
3. Put thematic material together in such a way that the strongest poem is last in the sequence.

Now read the Key Points from Chapter Five

KEY POINTS FROM CHAPTER FIVE

ACQUIRING PERFORMANCE SKILLS II

- Consider all the skills needed to add professionalism to the delivery of the poems: always have a sense of the dramatic in this.

- Work on characters to add more dramatic sense to what you do.

- Plan sequences carefully, noting length, variety and thematic links

- Research the setting and audience carefully: develop a 'feel' for a place

Now turn to Chapter Six

6

ACQUIRING PERFORMANCE SKILLS I

Without expecting any absolute, polished, acting skills, it is still possible to work on aspects of your projections of the written word, and this chapter deals with ways of perfecting this element in your performance.

Confidence first

Before any thoughts on how you are to project your voice and personality, consider the basic need for confidence. What exactly does that word imply in this particular context? In many cases, it is defined as simply having the 'bottle' to stand up and read your work. In its least admirable form, it might simply entail a shout or a rant. The recent growth of interest in the Poetry Slam idea has celebrated performance poetry in such a way that all-comers compete and the stress may easily be placed on power, immediacy and noise. There are more subtle aspects of what is meant by confidence. These are some aspects of how this applies to poetry-reading:

- being certain about why you do it

- having a clear idea of the reception/ effects

- using aspects of your own personality

- feeling comfortable in taking on a role

All these things are concerned with your sure grasp of why you are performing. For instance, you need to decide how far you will project a stance. The stance you take is the establishment of an attitude; reflect on what gestures, digressions, explanations, rapport with the audience etc. you want to achieve. The sum of these will be a useful gauge of your desired projection of a visible attitude to the listeners.

Learn by watching and logging

Clearly, when you start preparing a persona - an extension of yourself who is to be 'the performer' you are influencing both the character of your writing and the image, the public identity which people will form. Therefore, one of the best preparatory moves to make is to study some popular and established performers. But first, what about the particular sub-form within the whole blanket term, 'Performance poetry'? In other words, there are almost as many categories as performers. Note, for instance, these classifications:

light humour
surreal, imagist.
social commentary
autobiographical
discourse-centred

One only has to compare, say, John Hegley with Benjamin Zephaniah to notice that one performer will concentrate on the power and attraction of the discourse itself - as in the music accompaniment and the accent/dialect/patois used as part of the delivery. Others will read rather than perform - almost eclipsing the personality of the writer.

But there are plenty of masters of the art to study and learn from. Linton Kwesi Johnson and John Cooper Clarke for instance, represent two aspects of the appeal of social commentary mixed with a personal, highly individuated style. What can be learned from these, as an example of this process? From Johnson, it has to be the insistence of repetitions and refrains, with the marked rhythms of a specific non-standard language. With Clarke, it is again an accent, but the imposition of a certain sceptical, wry attitude creates a universal effect of commentary (as in *Majorca* in which Clarke can be seen commenting on materialism and a secular society, or simply celebrating an ingredient of modernity).

In a practical sense, what can be done with such study? These are some ways of working:

- listen to recordings and learn from word-play such as pun, repetition and wit.

- summarise the use of balanced and sequenced material

- note how a set or sequence is composed.

- list the varieties of linking devices used

- compare the delivery to aspects of lyrical singing etc.

The process will not be a short one, but it does force you to take note of the planning involved in even the shortest performance. After all, there is little that has not been done in performance. There are even some ad-lib artists around, some poets who work with spontaneous expression or digressive delivery.

Studying radio performers

There is a great deal to be learned from comparing poetry written for radio with poetry for stage performance. For example, in the Radio Four series, *Stanza*, Simon Armitage profiled several poets who exemplified the spectrum of available forms and genres. But poems specially written for radio illustrate an aspect which anyone can work on: this is the atmospheric effect. Consider a poem written for this medium, with a narrative content, drawing on autobiography and on sound-patterns and so on. What might it involve? Some possibilities are:

street-sounds
traffic
inner voices
varying registers of language in use
snatches of films/songs/ t.v. etc.

There is a lot to learn from here. Your poem for performance needs far more than the rhythms of the voice if it is to be distinctive. One illustrative example of this could be the use of interfusing registers: that is, using a range of voices, accents and discourses to dramatise what you read out. This is an example of a poem with such devices, and it is part of a poem written for radio:

from Intimate *Disclosures*

'Raaaaaam   raaaaam the traffic says,
whining its hatred at the November morning.
In her head the last dregs of a row,
a breakfast spit. All over a wrong word.
You lousy pig, you belong in a sty...
And 'Clement for this time of year in the North'
the radio crackles out into her skull'

If a writer can transfer some of these effects from the page to the airwaves or the stage, then a certain natural use of language as it actually exists can be commandeered for delivery. Use what is already there. In a popular poem which is clearly for reading aloud, the writer uses the 'Walk... Don't walk' of the American street (Adrian Henri) and in a sense, this approach is like the usual idea of 'found' poetry - the assembled language of the world as it presents data for your observation or your notebook.

The radio poem, of course, also has other resources to hand, but many of these can be incorporated into a reading. Such devices as echoes, sound-effects, choral sounds and so on, can be used in 'live' performance just as effectively.

Non-verbal elements

All such non-verbal elements are only difficult when it comes to relating them to your specific needs. Look at your own writing and ask what other dimensions could add drama and immediacy. An example might be like this:

Poetic subject - a motorway services/restaurant
Verbal elements - a refrain, a descriptive passage, a lyrical section, dialogue
non-verbal elements - traffic noise/ chatter/ buzzer/ machinery/ arcade games etc.
Technique: Intersperse words and effects, alternate description with dialogue.

But your own body and movements are also a part of the whole performance too. Use clothes, image and projection carefully. Every detail will be noticed by someone. So your appearance is important in this. A poet might pretend to smoke all the way through - or actually smoke - and use the breathing and 'dragging' process to keep the pace of delivery and add links. Every grimace and movement provides an intermission between poems.

Now read the Key Points from Chapter Six

KEY POINTS FROM CHAPTER SIX

ACQUIRING PERFORMANCE SKILLS I

Be sure about the sources of your need to perform

Note and understand your aims in the method of projection

Study established performers and take from them any aspects of technique,
even small details - turning them into your own artistic forms.

Itemise and learn all non-verbal additions to your performance

Now turn to Chapter Seven

7

ACQUIRING PERFORMANCE SKILLS II

Now the focus shifts to those fundamental abilities with handling language: the reading of syntax in terms of following the needs of an optimal reading - making the most of the 'flat' text on the page.

Reading aloud-narrative

So, at last you have planned everything around the text, but in the end, the acid test is in the projection and interpretation of what you have written. The poem is an assemblage of all kinds of meanings, all delivered to the reader through complex intonation patterns. One only has to read a technically very taut poem such as a sonnet to see how just one variant reading out of three can change the whole poem totally. Even one wrong intonation across a few syllables can change meaning. For these reasons, it helps to back to basic facts about the poem on the page and the poem as read or performed. Think of a poem, perhaps, as a tree: unmoved until the breeze of each reading. The degree to which the wind blows on the tree will change its outline, its movement and the angle of its stance.

The best way to illustrate how a performance re-creates a poem from the page is to use an example. Suppose this short poem from a sequence of three was read aloud: read this first.

Wives Recall

1. It was dead in our street
    in the years after the war.
    Mother never went to church again.
    Not after that; her heart died.
    Like twenty young men in one street.
    They talk about the Bradford Pals.
    What about the Pudsey Wives?
    They all joined up together as well.
    Grandma said, the Wondrous Regiment of Women.

Notice that everything here depends on the monologue quality of the voice. There is a story to tell, and like all good stories, it unravels slowly, with expectation. The listener should not expect any reference to the contrast between the men who died and the other 'regiment' back home. The italics on the word *they* is the first emphatic to push towards that contrast being political - so making a simple poem of statements into one that invites thoughts about gender, power and the bonds of local togetherness in adversity.

In a traditional 'reading aloud' of the poem, there would be little room for much else in the delivery, but in performance, you need the utmost drama and feeling from the simplicity. The emotive phrases such as 'her heart died' clearly demand a slow tempo, but much of the poem could be read in very different ways over several readings. One argument that insists that the above poem needs some other ingredient - that it is in some ways incomplete - is that there may not be a suggestion of a definitive reading. In other words, poets need to think about the scope for variety in each poem they write for performance.

What are the guidelines for reading narratives? Much may be learned from folksong and ballads. The bothy ballads, or individual singers of ballads such as Luke Kelly singing *The Rare old Times* with the Dubliners, give some help. That simple folk narrative tradition in singers such as Ewan MacColl and Anne Briggs gives some help. The success lies in the bare narrative, without much ornamentation. But in a more modern context, as in Murray Lachlan Young's contemporary stories (such as 'Simply everyone's taking cocaine') the delivery needs a dramatic tone and a conceived persona - in short, an act, a display of the attitude behind the poem.

It is difficult to provide a checklist for such skills, but this is a beginning:
1. Read your narrative poems several times, noting the phrases that carry the 'plant' of the real meaning.
2. Experiment with varying pace and time the readings
3. Consider 'voices' and accents etc. for certain sections.
4. Keep them short!

Reading aloud: drama
What makes the dramatic presence of a reading? Again, reference to a specific poem and reading might help. This is a poem that has been read several times at readings:

The Giftie Gi' Us
(An eclogue)
Damon: Off the peg but great style
        This is a classy suit, top-notch.
Phyllis: Wish he'd lay off for a while.
        I can smell pee around his crotch.
Damon: Well, I love this aftershave,
        and the beard's shaping up -adds some life.
Phyllis: Ah, gross smell! Must be called RAVE
        and that hairy face - looks fifty-five.
Damon: It's time to ask her to dinner.
        A quiet meal by candlelight for two.
Phyllis: He thinks he's on a winner.
        Think I'll hide a while in the ladies' loo.

This is a parody of a classical poem, an eclogue, in which two rural shepherds talk love. Here, the names echo such names on that conventional form. The alternating rhymes and the changes from one tone to another give a comic mode to the whole thing. In performance, though, the reader needs to give the lines in two voices, or obviously, have two different voices. Despite these basics, the poem still needs some other quality: a tempo and a sense of timing.

   The dramatic sense in poetry reading means a sense of certainty and confidence about how to read in such a way that the point is made subtly or strongly, according to form and to context. In the above poem, the words giving the rhymes, such as 'rave' and crotch' use the technique of bathos - moving sharply from the sublime to the ridiculous - for the effect. But there are hundreds of options open to you.

Clearly, in a serious or satirical poem, there is a need to put most emphasis on the clarity of sound, and on ensuring that the words carrying the emotional or ideological weight are heard by everyone. Timing and sensitivity to the mood of the audience play a part in this.

These are the basic items for a checklist in maintaining the dramatic in what you read:

• Read at the right pace to match the meaning and form.

• Speak clearly, taking time with every syllable. Don't contract words too much.

• Be sure that all rhymes and contrasts are perfectly obvious and prominent.

• Vary the mood and attitude

• Use movements and complementary gestures well but sparingly

How to find positive feedback
With all these considerations taken into account, it is time to think about the urgent and constant need for feedback. How does a poet find this? In many cases, it is simply trial and error. You try out the material on small and select audiences. You meet with other poets and performers and listen to each other's work. In a university for instance, you could join a writing group and start circulating writing for comments. In courses on

writing poetry, often run locally, similar things can be done. The important point is to try to find honest and useful responses as you go along. Not everyone has the chance to test an audience. In some instances, it may be best to simply be bold and try material out 'cold' so to speak.

But the poetry organisations and societies provide the best platform. There are several organisations listed in Barry Turner's *Writers' Handbook* (Macmillan), which is annual and up-dated. Even if you start at the local level, and read to small groups in college or at arts centres, WEA courses and so on, at least this provides immediate response, and gives you a chance to practise and perfect all the small secondary skills you need in performance.

Confidence is the primary consideration, however, and preliminary recording and listening to your reading and delivery of lines will prepare you for most responses. The fact is that only you know the material intimately, and all success is in your hands. There has to be preparation and research done.

Varying readings
With the above points in mind, it makes sense to experiments with varying readings of your poems. A well-documented example of this is in the case of Henry Reed's very much anthologised poem *The Naming of Parts,* in which we have two distinct voices - one of a sergeant giving rifle-loading instructions, and one of the private and his own interior reflections. Reed gives scope for plenty of wordplay, such as the dual meanings of

'spring' - in the season and in the catch in a gun's mechanism. Reed, interestingly, did not prefer the reading which uses two distinct voices. But a recording available commercially and read by Dylan Thomas clearly projects two voices.

The same kind of decisions will be open to you. Trial and adventure in these things is the only way to find your preference. Yet it is possible to find the best interpretations by chance, so why not use any other poets and writers in your group, class etc. to read aloud and maybe find new things in your poems?

The editing process usually brings out such possibilities; only by trying different syntax and word-selection will the right form be found. A useful way to work on a performance poem in the early stages of composition is to write in these three phases; each one is experimental and the differences will bring out important choices:

stage one:
Write the idea as prose, in ordinary sentences, not heightened for effect.
stage two:
Write in free verse or in blank verse
free: without and specific metrical rhythm or rhyme.
blank verse - unrhymed iambic pentameter, that is with a stress-pattern as follows -
u/ u/ u/ u/ u/   (unstressed syllable followed by stressed syllable X 5)

stage three

Try a rhyme-scheme in some lines - alternate or in any position.

The point in doing this is that you will sense the strengths of each version and settle on the best form for performance. By reading aloud, and even recording each version, the feel for the natural expression of the idea will emerge.

Now read the Key Points from Chapter Seven

KEY POINTS FROM CHAPTER SEVEN

ACQUIRING PERFORMANCE SKILLS II

- Read your work several times before any final decisions about style and form.

- Stress the drama and narrative elements in your poems. Audiences want both, as often as possible, in performance.

- Make sure you find some feedback from other practitioners before reading to an audience.

- Experiment with writing the same theme in different forms, to find the most satisfactory one *for you*, of course.

Now turn to Chapter Eight

8

WORKING WITH OTHERS

In many cases, the whole idea of performing or reading poetry aloud, is never conceived as a single-person enterprise. This chapter looks at the advantages of working with other poets.

The advantages of collaboration

A study of some performance poets indicates that there may not be a clear black and white divide between the two approaches of either single or group performances. The very popular Ian McMillan, for instance, started his career in earnest with a group called *Circus of Poets*. In the early eighties, they presented a dynamic performance, each one of four poets integrating into a certain slick and fast series of deliveries. The group image was strong (sometimes a bright red tee-shirt and plenty of vaudeville). Now, Ian most often reads or performs on his own. He has developed a mix of stand-up comedy which relies on anecdotal surrealism and poetry. In this case, it would be difficult to argue as to which version of Ian McMillan was the most successful in this context.

But for most of us, it may be worthwhile considering the benefits of teaming up and working with other performers. Some of the obvious advantages can easily be listed:

1. Instant variety for the audience.
2. A sure objective for each individual - you know where you fit in.
3. A greater chance of creative gambits and accidental arrival at technique etc.

But there are other factors here. An example might be the need to look at the limitations of your corpus. If you tend to write with a very narrow range of topics and styles, then it may be that you could add a very fruitful extension of what you do if you work with another writer.

Ask yourself what you need to perfect the necessary variety into the act. After all, there is a lot to decide in terms of the final impact you wish to leave with the audience. Does your writing tend to be persuasive, polemic, descriptive, imagistic and so on? Look closely at what you have written so far and decide on whether or not you tend to have dominant categories of themes and preoccupations. Of all the potential benefits of working with others, which might be your specific gain? There could be several considerations here, but these are common scenarios:

1. Your work tends to be dealing with the past.
So some of your styles and topics are reflective, nostalgic? Clearly,

working with someone more contemporary would be a help. It might an add currency of up-to-date-feeling and interchange with the audience.

2. Your work is almost all autobiographical, close-focused. The range narrow.

Clearly, you need a wider, panoramic scope. Maybe a writer who writes social commentary or satire would work well, in contrast, to your writing.

3. You tend to write with high expression, but your work is not 'literary' and looks superficial on the page.

Now, this one demands some thought. Do you want to counterbalance the two varieties, and why? Some poets, notably, Murray Lachlan Young, John Cooper Clarke and John Hegley, have an instinct for a natural progression but always within their usual set or sequence. You might want to develop your own kinds of variety inside quite narrow limits, and maybe any partnership is not required. A positive way to look at this is to monitor reactions to what you think are your strongest themes and work on whether or not they need broadening and complementary performance.

Complementing and using themes

Naturally, the real advantage of working with others is the contrast of two styles that you gain. Notice the success of readings, even in cases in which there is simply reading aloud rather than performance, which place three poets together at random. Just the effect of three voices and appearances is enough to suggest variety.

A brief checklist of the subjects covered by most poetry will alert the writer to creative possibilities. A recent article in Good Housekeeping magazine (Nov.1997) suggests that women poets aspiring to be part of the burgeoning scene in which Sophie Hannah and Selima Hill have succeeded should just'buy a notebook ' and get in on the action. The piece implies that any observation is potential poetry. So the 'subject' of poetry is now anything at all. But the dominant areas are still love, death, parting, loss, social commentary and autobiographical moment-capture.

What is interesting from a performance viewpoint is that the newest type of stage poetry is one that adopts voices and personae. The link with rock and jazz, or even rap and reggae lyrics, is being made, and therefore traditional subjects are perhaps under attack. Certainly traditional delivery is very much criticised as being staid and tedious - too predictable.

But it is easy to argue that the usual approach of keeping to themes so that the audience sees a certain structure and cohesion is still effective. The best way to maximise success here is to complement your basic material with something visual. Note these common techniques:

- back-projection

- choral devices

- semi-musical or dance devices

- the rant - a maintained monotone assault or invective

At the latest vogue-event, the Poetry Bash, as at Bristol and Cheltenham in 1997, the pace and the competition perhaps encourages the more dynamic aspects of intonation and rhythmic delivery - even into quite excited, possessed states suggesting ad lib style.

Of the items in the above list, maybe the first and last are the least exploited. The use of back-projection, simply using illustrations on an overhead projector, for instance, can put photographic images behind you as you read, just as if a projector was clicking into synchronised delivery with your poems. You could even have an image given for each section or stanza of a poem.

The last one, implying that you project almost as if the feeling dominates, at shouting level, presents an interesting debate. This concerns the sheer imposition of sound and presence into the audience. At the least dynamic level, you read the poem quietly and with feeling; but there seems to be a 'Beaufort Scale' applied to readings, going up to the stentorian levels of shouting and screaming. Think seriously about the effect and impact when using such approaches. Again, as a complementary device rather than a dominating one, this might be most effective. The American poet, La Loa, for instance, gave a reading a few years ago, in which a long and very radical, political poem was read. She modulated the reading so that when she raised levels, we were clear why this was done. That Beat-originated approach to reading tended to place the emphasis on a highly-individuated response to experience, and there are signs that this is returning into fashion, largely through the renewed interest in the late Alan Ginsberg and in the continuing popularity (and cult status) of Jack Kerouac.

To sum up, the suggestion is that a poet needs both depth and thematic interest in a reading. These are best achieved by stark simplicity and a suggestion of the honesty and directness of the projection of the words. A reflection on the way in which television presents a poem will consolidate this. During the voting for the Nation's Favourite Poem in 1997, dramatic reading and one simple image was effective enough to give the impact.

Dynamics!
Despite all these suggestions of rather cautious and often corporate planning strategies, in the end, it is the poet's contact with the feeling and ultimately with the experience or response behind the poem that makes for success. If you have never done this, now is the time to ask these questions about your work:

1. Do you write on impulse, from a quick response to life?
2. Are you largely a poet of ideas rather than feelings?
3. Do you want to create your own style totally -or settle for a derivative one?
4. Do you instinctively act or simply read a poem?

All these points cover the issue of how a poem, in the life of its reading, suggests absolute authenticity of experience. The point is that each reading is like resuscitating a corpse. How do you make the words stay 'alive'? Each reading is a potentially a revisiting of the experience itself.

Use any strategy that works to keep that authentic feel to every reading. Clearly, only a certain proportion of your work will lend itself to this. There are undeniably a large number of poems which are simply descriptive lists of images, and their scope for such revitalisation is very limited.

Ultimately, these factors will help you decide on whether to work with others or not.

Now read the Key Points from Chapter eight

KEY POINTS FROM CHAPTER EIGHT

WORKING WITH OTHERS

- Think about the benefits to you of working alone or with other poets

- Decide whether or not a collaboration would add significant elements to your performance

- Study types of complementing a poetry reading and decide on which suits your style.

- Be aware of the impetus to writing that underlies your work, and keep that, even when working with others.

Now turn to Chapter Nine.

9

ORGANISING YOURSELF

There are many aspects of writing poetry which have little to do with art and a lot to do with common sense, planning and management. If you take your writing seriously, then this is worth as much attention as the art of writing itself.

Networking and promotion
In today's society, art is generally information-led and created or mediated by market forces. Anyone wanting to survive as an artist, even in terms of a part-time occupation, needs to be aware of competition and of the information channels available. The idea of networking is not a new concept, but it has totally revolutionary connotations for any writer wanting to actually earn some money and reach a certain status.

For example, note just how many people are writing poetry now. Even the small presses are inundated with scripts. We live in an environment in which so many people see writing as a branch of the leisure industry that writing courses exist on the Internet, in CDROM programmes, in distance-learning forms and of course, as part of courses, both large and small. Thousands enter the National Poetry Competition, and there is a booming industry in books for writers - like the present one.

What can you learn from this situation? If you take your writing seriously, then you have one huge advantage as someone who wishes to write performance poetry. There is not so much competition here. Most poets still see poetry as a lonely, reader -based art. It is still intellectualised and still defined largely as the province of academics and critics. Certain large publishers still dominate the market, in the context of kudos and of finance. But performance poetry is just beginning to branch out, to have a widespread cultural impact. If you want to be part of that, then think about these needful measures in a world where self-promotion is a necessity:

- Work around a diary all the time.

- Keep records of all contacts

- Attend short courses, conventions and conferences

- Cultivate your local Arts Association

- Give readings locally and start small-scale

Notice that all this hinges on personal contacts. Unlike poetry written for small magazines or anthologies, performance writing depends for its success on people working and planning together, and on the recognition of a specific audience. The established reading circuits are the best place to begin, or within a college or university. Join one of the larger national groups (see the list of addresses at the end of this book). Read widely and study professionals. There are some books on the market, which anthologise performance poetry, notably edited by Paul Beasley of 57 Productions.

Essential paperwork

Once you start having readings booked, and make contacts with other writers and groups, you will need to start recording/logging systems to keep organise and monitor everything you do in this new professional career. The basics are these:

1. Keep a master -diary with all addresses and events recorded.
2. Up-date addresses of contacts.
3. Make use of the Internet to maintain interest and information.
4. Join and participate in events. Literature festivals are a useful start, even in small fringe events.
5. Keep accounts of fees and expenses - methodically.
6. Invest in the essential reference books (see resources section)

Above all, these records should start with submissions and editorial feedback. If you do submit to magazines or competitions etc. then log the submissions carefully. Keep a cuttings file and a feedback file of all critical reports from readers, editors and so on. The aim is to check your progress. But you can keep a checklist of more particular things also. A really worthwhile critical log is the answer. In other words, track the performance life of each of your best poems. You might note the reception it receives, and whether or not it has a repeatedly positive response. The same applies to the less successful poems as well. Even poems that have a personal significance may not be effective in performance. Do not continue with them.

This is one practical way of working in this context:

1. Use a large notebook and use a page for each poem.
2. Monitor the success of each poem - in terms of reception when read editors opinions from magazines and so on.
3. Re-file and order according to the sequence of reading that brings the best results.
4. Keep the poems in a display-book with a hard cover for durability.

Finally, notice the common practice now of using all the following communication-channels in professional work:
address/business cards
flyers
posters with a photo
a press-cuttings/reviews file
letters file

All of these have been shown to pay off. Keep yourself in the public eye; keep active. Write and phone producers and editors; circulate your promotional materials. Be at events.

Communication factors
There are three applications of this phrase in performance poetry.
1. The maintenance of letters etc. with other colleagues.

2. Personal /inter- relational.
3. Internal communication in your own systems.

What these all have in common is that they stem from the awareness of poetry as a communal art; increasingly now, it may be argued, poetry is impinging on other parallel arts, and your communication methods have to keep up. Maybe in a short time, all booking and promotions in this sphere will be done by E-Mail and the Net. But at the moment, one thing is certain - there is now a whole range of outlets for performance, as opposed to the traditional poetry society or local college writing-group. Amateurism is increasingly marginalised.

With all this in mind, the point is that all areas of communication need to be streamlined. The central one, that of writing letters, is still the axis of the most productive exchanges, and a meeting face-to-face is surely still irreplaceable as the best basis for an understanding. Do them all; be active on all levels. But most of all, concentrate on the effectiveness of your voice and appearance.

One case study will illustrate the importance of all this. My character -poet J.Arthur Bowler once read in the bar/restaurant of a college. The audience had just had a meal and were relaxing in the bar. There were perhaps 40 people there. My poet walked in, after a short announcement, and leaned against the corner of the bar. He had about six poems to read and the rest was 'patter'.

I had not researched the event. In fact, I was preceded by a national bagpipe champion, and I believe that the audience were ready for some peace. I assailed them with an intrusive Yorksire yammer and some salacious tales in between the poems. It was only a partial success. The response was fair, but not enthusiastic.

I had not researched, not asked enough questions beforehand. This is such an elementary error, and it was certainly a learning experience. The minimum checklist of what to do as good communication would be this:

Do
Check on facilities
Draw a rough sketch of the area and stage
Be aware of intrusive noise
Use the space to its maximum

.

The point about noise is so important. I once organised a reading at which Iain Crichton Smith came to a rugby club to talk and read. Behind a partition, there were a few games machines in operation. The sound was not very loud, but Iain was a quiet speaker and did not project very forcefully.

Now turn to the Key Points from Chapter Nine

KEY POINTS FROM CHAPTER NINE

ORGANISING YOUSELF

- Put great emphasis on your public persona. Advertise and promote at all occasions.

- Maintain accurate and regular records of everything you do - from meetings to courses and performances.

- Work on good communications at every level.

Now turn to Chapter Ten

10

RESOURCES

Having decided on making this form of writing your special concern, the need for a wide range of resources is necessary; this covers everything from reference books to organisations who support and encourage performance poetry.

The need for up-dating
The central resource is one of your own making: maintaining your address-book and also your own records and notes pertaining to potential material for writing. For instance, your thematic material will need constant sustenance; you might build on photo-files or increase your 'model' writing based on favourite forms and conventions. Whatever your taste in terms of preferred audience and location, there will always be a need for change. A study of the career of any poet in this respect will soon demonstrate the truth of this. Roger McGough is an example. His basic formula for performance has always been a reliance on a delivery based on a very specific accent; this has been a studied, overstated Liverpudlian. He has made the colloquial and regional his own province, but mixed it with a neo-Romanticism. Several of his poems mix techniques based on Symbolist works with North of England subjects.

As his career has advanced, he has tried several new idioms, all around the basic approach of interweaving very soft-centred, human interest poems with a melancholy and reflective view of particular experience. When he takes on a huge theme, it is from an intuitive angle. Performance poetry can open up possibilities for making innovations in conventional form. Even a simple technique like McGough's habit of running words into others makes for a certain glib and slick effect. Simple word-play can add details.

All this is a way of seeing just how performance poetry seems to attract anything quirky, individual and wayward. The notion of writing for listeners, as opposed to readers, leads the writing towards a central dynamic, which relies on each poet's personal idiosyncracies of expression.

For these reasons, there needs to be a monitoring process of your habits of reading and delivery. Variety and the aesthetic attraction of a voice's intonations have to be constantly scrutinised. So what should you do in this area?

1. Video some performances. Check any positive and negative factors. Treat the whole exercise as an art, not a hobby or a *jeu d'esprit*.
2. re-read and consider your resources files occasionally. Reject anything stale. Always build in new work from everyday observation.

3. Use contemporary reference. If social commentary is your interest, then take lines and phrases from the media etc. for use ironically or as chants, refrains and so on.

4.   Up-date all addresses and publications.

The scope of potential sources
What are the sources of your writing? It is never a waste of time to remind oneself of the differences between writing for speech as opposed to page. The nature of a performed poem will always be alive, always open to revision and adaptation. So the sources of your work should also continue to expand. Variety is the key. The mix of contemporary themes and changeless, universal experience will always produce interesting results. If one accepts that a performed poem will not draw on anything more than the compelling sense of *now*, of the occasion, then using what is to hand will be part of the creative process. In a recent television film based on Ian McMillan's visit to Mexico (Nov.1997, *Yorkshire T.V.*) he used the idea of children's school and street rhymes to make a point about the insistence and centrality of such rhythms in the adhesion of communal sense. It relied only on a beat and a set of stressed syllables. The language and meaning were almost dispensable.

Similarly with any notion of selecting sources according to pre-conceived ideas of social importance or of intellectual significance. A classic example of flexibility and change is the work of Bob Cobbing. His performances using the body and syllabic sounds were an attempt to change our perceptions of the communal functions of poetry. In the sixties and seventies, he was reclaiming poetic discourse from the study and the bookshelf. In each individual way, a performer must use anything that will establish the communal sense - shock, rage, ranting, monotony, elegy, and so on, into every available discourse.

Courses, societies and outlets.
The best source for this material is in the pages devoted to poetry in Barry Turner's annual *The Writer's Handbook* (Macmillan). This gives information about organisations who would encourage and support your work. The most significant in a national context, are the following:
Apples and Snakes, Unit A11, Hatcham Mews Business Centre, Hatcham Mews Park, London SE14 5QA
57 productions, Paul Beasley, Effingham Road, Lee Green, London SE12 8NT
The Living Poets Society, Dragonheart Press, 11, Memin Road, Allestree, Derby DE22 2NL
The National Convention of Poets and Small Presses, Iron Press, 5, Marden Terrace, Cullercoats, North Shields, Northumberland NE30 4PD
The Poetry Business, The Studio, Byram Arcade, Westgate, Huddersfield, West Yorks. HD1 1ND
The Poetry Society, 22, Betterton Street, London WC2H 9BU

In addition to these, the local groups of poets around the country and the literature festivals are a useful source for events, contacts and promotional initiatives. The regional arts organisations are the place to start, and again, these are listed in Turner's book.

Outlets for readings are easily listed:

- local colleges and universities

- small groups of enthusiasts

- local branches of the WEA

- arts association programmes and funded activities

- literature festivals

Courses in writing poetry for performance are quite rare. It is still a form of poetry which is winning a place in academic contexts. But the starting point for any poet wanting to study and learn the art systematically should go on from this introduction to a course if possible. Full-time degree courses may have components that involve such things, but the best place to start is to contact the **Arvon Foundation**, Lumb Bank, Heptonstall, Hebden Bridge, West Yorks. HX7 6DF. Another useful organisation for this is the **National Association of Writers in Education**, PO Box 1, Sheriff Hutton, York YO6 7YU

Essential reference: books and magazines
This is a selected list of books useful for the skills of writing poetry:
Michael Baldwin The *Way to Write Poetry* (Elm Tree Books) 1988
Doris Corti Writing *Poetry* (Thomas and Lochar) 1995
Peter Finch *How to Publish your Poetry* (Allison and Busby) 1989

Graham Mort The *Experience of Poetry* (Open University) 1991

Peter Sansom Writing *Poems* (Bloodaxe) 1994

Stephen Wade Writing *and Publishing Poetry* (How To) 1996

Anthologies

Some useful collections of performance poems:

The Mersey Poets - McGough, Henri, Patten (Penguin) 1995

Paul Beasley Hearsay: *Performance Poems Plus* (Red Fox) 1995

Ian McMillan Against *the Grain* (Nelson) 1989

Poets on Compact Disc/cassette

Some useful performances to listen to and study are:

John Cooper Clarke Disguise *in Love* (Epic)

John Hegley Hearing *with Hegley* (BBC)

Kerouac Kicks, *joy, darkness* (RCD)

Linton Kwesi Johnson on *Reggae Greats* (IMCD)

Magazines of interest

Freelance Writing and Poetry, Tregeraint House, Zennor, St.Ives, Cornwall TR26 3DB

Quartos BCM Writer, 27 Old Gloucester Street, London WC1N 3XX

Stand, 179,Wingrove Road, Newcastle upon Tyne, NE4 9DA

Writers News PO Box 4, Nairn, Scotland IV 12 4HU

Writing Magazine, PO Box 4, Nairn, Scotland IV12 4HU

These magazines contain articles on specific writing skills, genres and markets for work. They also update all professional writers on matters of copyright, new initiatives, courses, and publications.

11

INNOVATION AND EXPERIMENT

We live in a time in which an artist of any kind is under more and more pressure to adapt – in some cases to adapt and survive. Marginal art will often be marginalised even more. Poetry has had to struggle to stay in the public arena in English writing since we lost the strong oral tradition. Therefore with every day that passes poets interested in performance of any kind need to look for new ways of putting their art and narratives into places were there will be an audience, however small.

Relating to the Oral Tradition

Paradoxically, much of what we think of as performance poetry does have roots in the art of storytelling, but when the 'page poetry' with an intellectual bias gained some prominence, the oral elements became harder to see. For instance, if we imagine the typical 'poetry reading' then the sense of that sharing of experience has many aspects of what would be found, for instance, in the telling of fairy and folk tales around the peat fire in rural Ireland:

- A closeness to the shared language of reader and audience

- A small-scale interaction

- The rapport between teller and listener, with facial expression as a guide.

- Reference to a shared social experience and register of language

Unfortunately there are also some aspects of the oral tradition which may only very rarely be found in the conventional poetry reading, such as a recognition on the part of the poet that his audience share certain assumptions about a position on perceived ideological frameworks applied to everyday experience. For this latter reason the reputation of 'poetry readings' as being elitist and pretentious has, it has to be said, sometimes been justified.

When performance poetry came along, there were some steps taken to take note of that special rapport in storytelling, and it is worth reflecting on that link if a writer is contemplating an attempt to switch to a more populist or accessible poetic voice. At the centre of this is the immediacy of the contact between teller and listener. If we think of the ancient tradition of capturing the audience's attention, as when a gesture or a single word gains a sharp silence in a hubbub of noise, that focus is what is needed.

A shared story is to be a narrative open to being reworked and embellished, as the story will either be known by everyone concerned or will be something told with a familiar and comfortable style and vocabulary, as in a stand-up comedy routine. So with a performance poem, first the attention of listeners is essential and second, the immediate accessibility of the poem has to be declared.

A storyteller will use one of a variety of techniques for this: maybe a musical instrument will be used or something surprising – maybe visual such as a scarf or something held in the hand, colourful or attractive. I have seen one storyteller use a small drum or an ocarina, for instance. More simple and direct is a 'patter' based on comfort (the old radio *Listen with Mother*- 'are you sitting comfortably? Then I'll begin'). Formulaic statements or questions such as 'Are you all in a story/poetic mood then?' or 'Who's up for a poem with a story to tell?' A performance poem needs to be part of a whole 'package' today. That means a poet has to pay attention to his/her appearance of course, and certainly to the voice used. It might seem odd, but on experience I would say that the template of a story told to children is a useful one here: that is because all performance relies for success on communal ease and imaginative escape. A performance poet is competing with other compulsively dramatic forms of art and narrative such as stand-up, circus, song and dance.

What in former times was a place on the fringe, hoping for someone to notice your skill is now something more ambitious – if you want to succeed in this of course. There are no half measures. The oral tradition is something that acts as a paradigm as well as a resource, naturally. There is no point in simply telling a poem and therefore being a storyteller rather than a poet. So what is the difference? Arguably, performance takes place in storytelling, it goes without saying, but that the addition of poetry creates other expectations. What are these?

The Difference of Performance
Clearly, performance poetry suggests the opposite of a storytelling place: it is taken to be louder, more forthright, more disturbing or bold. That may or may not be true, but the point is that there are poetic features and they differ from storytelling. To understand this difference, we need to think about the specific interaction that goes on in that context. Think about a poetry event in a pub, for instance. The poet or poets establish the mood and the aims at the very first point of contact with the audience. Their first words and actions define what the promise of the performance is: are we talking about pure entertainment, laugh after laugh? Or is the promise one of a mix of serious, thought-provoking work interspersed with light relief? If the aim is zany anarchistic Pythonesque comedy, then that will be plain. As with all comedy, the problem then is to 'follow that.' But performance in terms of poetry has a particular quality of imaginative escape. What the poet is doing is:

- Inviting a journey into imagery and invention with a register of its own

- That register will be somewhere on the spectrum of serious – circus
- The words with usually tie into an established stance on life

- That stance will often be defined or suggested by appearance and voice.

The powerful mix of voice and appearance is the best clue to understanding what is needed to innovate, and that is the fundamental challenge of this art form.

Slams and Purses

The advent of the Poetry Slam has changed the face of performance poetry, and what this tells us is that the rise of amateurism is now complete. The art of globalism is one that welcomes the amateur, and lack of skill in a specific art is not necessarily a handicap. But of course, what can pass for poetry on the internet and in small self-produced booklets is not necessarily open to success when the words are lifted off the page. But the 'slam' finds a way around all this because it is all about spontaneity.

The idea is very simple: writers and performers turn up at a club or pub or university society and they read/perform their work in front of a fairly rowdy audience, and the reward is a purse – a small entry fee by each participant provides that. The winner takes all, or the three winners, whatever is arranged. Although this is open to anyone with the requisite courage, and in spite of the obvious drawbacks regarding quality, there is one great virtue of this concept, and that is that word *spontaneity*. It could be argued that spoken poetry, with its closeness to comic entertainment and monologue (as in the music hall) is better when it seems to be extempore. Even if it is not, that does not matter. The point is that is *seems* to be so.

I met a writer once who knew around thirty of his poems by heart. When eh spoke them, it gave him a truly pleasurable smile: he was sharing his words in a way very different from the equivalent reading aloud from a book. Somehow, he knew, without having to explain it, that he was giving you some words that were a part of him – integral to his verbal responses to the world, a part of himself in a deeper sense than if he had put a collection of poems into my hand and asked me to go and read them elsewhere.

That quality is something close to what is needed here. After all, a person is more openly immersed in his or her language if it flows orally – not studied, permanent, as in print. He may well have changed and embellished when he spoke his words – again, just as a professional storyteller does.

A slam needs a great deal of 'bottle ' of course. But it has to be stressed that there are few more effective ways of sounding out the responses to something one has written. The faces are there in front o the poet – maybe a little tipsy but also clearly i=either entertained or not.

All about Responses

In my creative writing courses, I often spend some time in a workshop situation merely practising and exploring the notion of 'getting a response' and that is every similar to what happens in a slam. Students are asked merely to write an opening paragraph, in any style or genre, and to try as hard as possible to write something that will guarantee a response when they read the piece aloud. The only constraint is that they must not use obscenities. We define what that means before writing, as it is, of course, a flexible concept.

What usually happens is that we have absurdity, savage satire, sheer grotesque revulsion (horror genre), sarcasm or self-deprecation. Reference to bathrooms and toilets is quite common, and of course, so is sex.. What we learn in these sessions is that a main element in that attempt to entertain is to revel in some artistic anarchy – to forget rules, even to the point of messing around with grammar, syntax and spelling. It also encourages a childish indulgence in poems that emerge in the vein of Lewis Carroll or A. A. Milne.

Innovation is Sheer Courage

Poets just starting out in performance may feel that these varieties of writing are too far away from the traditional 'slim lyric' or meditation. Maybe this is so, but I would argue that every writer has a range, however small that may be in some cases, so a profitable first step is to explore that part of your range of subjects and styles in which the voice and the delivery of meaning is most bold, most expressive and most courageous.

Courage is, after all, what performance needs as the deep basis of the activity: the sheer *hutzpah* of standing up and sharing personal language, working hard to transmute that into a communal one. Again, as with comedy, two things happen once you start:

(a) Everything clicks into place and the listeners are part of your vision of things.

(b) You miss the mark but you adapt in response to the faces and expressions you see.

People often think that a performer is so nervous and self-aware that the second action will be impossible. But all that can be said is that the art of performance poetry is one like stepping into the sea to bathe. The reaction to the very cold water will be a shock, but one adapts and soon swims in it, the mind elsewhere and the body moving spontaneously – and there is that key word again.

Now read the Key Points from chapter 11

KEY POINTS FROM CHAPTER ELEVEN
INNOVATION AND EXPERIMENT

- Study and reflect on the art of storytelling, seeing what can be learned.
- Consider the oral tradition and how to extract from it techniques that match what you wish to do in performance.
- Observe and reflect on a poetry slam and think about what it says about how people relate to poetry in everyday life rather than in the study.

Now turn to Chapter Twelve.

12

CASE STUDIES

There is no better way to see what the opportunities and scope of poetry in performance might be than to survey some of the successful performers on the scene today or in recent years. Although the very nature of the art is that it tends to be transient, ephemeral and sometimes following short trends, it is at least something always flexible and tends to be a form of narrative that allows for new faces. But it is hard to say why those writers who stayed in a prominent place in performance poetry did in fact succeed. The names of such poets that come to mind are Benjamin Zephaniah, John Agard, Adrian Mitchell, Roger McGough and Ian MacMillan; though a case could be made for many others.

What is intended in this chapter is an effort to describe some of the most individual achievements of perhaps lesser known poets and writers. The above list consists of poets who have done several things in writing, not really specialising in one 'compartment' of performance and some (such as McGough) would not even thing of themselves as 'performance' poets at all. But whatever the individual views of that are, the fact is that each of those offers more than a simple reading.

In my column on performance for *Writing Magazine* over the last few years, I have written about poets in many places along that spectrum of performance, some mixing words with other media; some working in collaborative ways and some prioritising poetry in the community and even documentary links in their projects. The following is a selection of the artists whose work has claims of being something we can learn from, something pushing boundaries.

Grass Roots: John Shepherd and Les Baynton

Here are two writers who show the way in making the most of sheer adventurous endeavour in following the joy of writing. John Shepherd is 'big in Berkshire.' His achievements and activities provide a case study in commitment and persistence. John was born in Dundee in 1944, then read Maths at Leeds University. He was a talented runner in his youth and almost made the Olympic team in 1968. He has done a great deal in his life, mostly very active things, not at all connected to poetry, on the surface at least. But as all writers know, experienced is never wasted when it comes to 'material.' In the 1970s he had his name in print for the first time in the local paper; but since then he has written travel articles and done his first novel.

The poetry came later. He says that he had performed the odd poem at a local folk club, but 'didn't take poetry seriously until 2003.' At the Allcomers Poetry Slam at Cheltenham he was successful in reaching the qualifiers both that year and the next. His list of credits since then show that he is going places. He won first prize at the Poole Literary festival in 2005, and went away with a silver cup. In Slough, his stamina saw him through a half-hour slot at Fenner Fest. John comments that some slam poetry is 'vulgar' and insist that he is happy to show anything he has written to his thirteen-year-old daughter.

John tries to get something positive out of disasters, as in these lines from My Operation, a poem facing up to the delicate subject of a vasectomy:

> *In 25 minutes or so, the doctor had another go.*
> *As his knife cut in again, I yelled at the familiar pain.*
> *Two students came to hold me tight,*
> *To make sure that I couldn't fight....'*

He can handle the insistent comic rhymes with as much dexterity as Pam Ayres at times, but for John the whole business is about a gig and a responsive audience. Why else would a man face up to a crowd of people out to make a row?

Les Baynton, on the other hand, shows all aspiring poets how to exploit the communal and convivial elements in reading and performing poetry. He leads a group and related publications called Pint pot Poets in Derby and he works in schools wherever he has a gig. On top of that he is a master as making a session go well, always full of life and inspiration. A former teacher (Headmaster in fact) he has the presence we need in this game. What he exemplifies is the 'MC' who reads and also involves others in writing and performing. His collections include *The Punch from Outer Space*, illustrated by Martin Wright, published by Pint Pot Poets.

What is outstanding about these two writers is that they illustrate the refreshing nature of performance poetry as something written generally with a front of intellectualism and density of linguistic texture in the writing. Les Baynton, for example, regularly arranges a poetry night and coaches beginners to read their work aloud at the Caerleon Writers' Holidays in Newport every summer. The turn-out is always hearteningly large and the word about poetry being cool is spreading, thanks to Les.

John Cooper Clarke and his Influence

There are some names on the performance poetry map who have made such an original contribution that they will always be a presence and an influence. One such name is John Cooper Clarke. He will always be the original punk poet for many and for some he will always be an entertainer, above fads and fashions. He has always adopted a wry stance in his commentaries on modern life, delivered with his sharp sense of irony and attack. For many poetry enthusiasts his early recording of the poem *Majorca* will always define his originality – a drawn-out northern accent full of sly comment and cheeky intonation.

Johnny Clarke was born in Salford in 1949. He started out in the Manchester folk clubs and then joined the Ferrets band with Rick Goldstraw. It is entirely in keeping with his art that he was originally aiming at being a stand-up comic; he has the energy and originality for that, but satirical verse and a microphone were waiting for him, his natural metier. His Manchester accent and powerful stage presence – black hair, long face and tight jeans – will be a hallmark. But the words he uses also have the impact, with or without a visual element.

To listen to his CDs is to experience a shock: a mix of musical styles, cleverly integrated into the poems, and a sleek, sharp delivery of puns and paradoxes, staggeringly original phrases and a liberal sprinkling of abuse. His lines such as 'I don't want to be nice' and 'a friend in need is a friend in debt' express the appeal very neatly. Add to that the deadpan voice and the changes of tone and mood as he goes through the repertoire, and we have a master: listen to the recordings and learn – or better still go to a performance. Even if some call him a cult artist, that's a cult that any performance poet needs to experience if not join.

Voices on Tape
There are so many excellent poets around that it is hard to select the most influential, but what can be done when starting out is to listen to the best from the past on tape. This can now be done very easily thanks to the Poetry Archive at www.poetryarchive.org and

we owe this in many ways to the Poet Laureate, Andrew Motion, who, as he recorded some of his own poems for Faber and Faber, commented that there was no comprehensive collection of poets' work on record over the years. The result of this is a unique library of recordings, launched in December, 2005, with almost 100 voices on record; the site was planned for five years, and as Andrew Motion has written: 'We intend to track down and add all the significant recordings we can find... if anyone has Hardy's voice in the attic, please tell us.'

The aim is to have a national resource for new poets and experienced campaigners alike, to establish a 'canon' of voices, so that the range is there for reference: everything from dialect to new urban intonations and slang. It is surely a resource for anyone wanting to know and listen to the best poetry recordings produced over the years.

Listening to poets performing their work is a much ignored part of the learning process. I feel that one of my formative experiences as a poet was listening to Seamus Heaney reading on a tape produced by Faber and Faber. The poems were from his first collection, *Death of a Naturalist* (1966) and these readings helped me to understand that the language of one's own local imaginative domain was acceptable – that we don't have to write like Tennyson or Brooke. I saw that there was no monopoly on the poetic voice in the metropolis, regardless of where a poet lives and works.

This new archive makes it easier for poets at all stages of their writing careers to listen and learn. After all, the imaginative centre of the art is in the spoken word and in how talented each individual is in expressing their won words in their own way. As Motion has said, there is a 'sound-sense' as well as a depth of meaning in a successful poem.

Conclusions

Thoughts about varieties of poets working in performance only lead to a certainty that there are really no rules in the art, only guidelines, things that make the breakthrough a little easier. But in the end, the axis between success or failure is always measured in the poet's own terms. There is a poet in Birmingham called Big Bren and he is something of a lesson to all: he and his group of like-minded enthusiasts want to stand up and read their work and make poetry cool everywhere. That is the heart of the enterprise. Ian MacMillan has taken poetry onto trains, into police-beats in Hull and into communities on the street in the north.

Performance poetry is naturally a stagey affair, but it does extend its considerable range into so many other areas of life that there is always room for new writers if their voice is different and commands attention in the right place at the right time and for the right audience. That could almost be a winning formula, but as all poets and writers gradually learn, that process of sounding out the potential audience is always a mix of sheer bravado, ridiculous self-belief and the most thorough preparation for the performance that can be done in the time available.

Now read the key points from chapter 12 overleaf

KEY POINTS FROM CHAPTER TWELVE
CASE STUDIES

- Read and listen to all kinds of poetic voices
- Explore all influential poets' work and find them in collections, on web sites and in archives
- Believe in your words and to the research

Now start reading, writing and performing and access your own words with honesty.